W9-BYE-959

STARS, PLANETS,
and Their Patterns

by Thomas K. Adamson

PEBBLE
a capstone imprint

Published by Pebble, an imprint of Capstone.
1710 Roe Crest Drive, North Mankato, Minnesota 56003
capstonepub.com

Library of Congress Cataloging-in-Publication Data is available on the Library of Congress website

ISBN: 9781666355000 (hardcover)
ISBN: 9781666355048 (paperback)
ISBN: 9781666355086 (ebook PDF)

Summary: What are stars? What are planets? Why are some stars brighter than others? Which planets can we see from Earth? Learn the answers to these questions and more and discover the science behind stars, planets, and their patterns.

Editorial Credits
Editor: Alison Deering; Designer: Sarah Bennett; Media Researcher: Svetlana Zhurkin; Production Specialist: Katy LaVigne

Image Credits
Shutterstock: Aphelleon, 4 (top left) and throughout, Dean Drobot, 21, Dima Zel, 10, elladoro, 7, imagedb, 20, Nowwy Jirawat, 1, Nurhuda Rahmadihan, 11, Ralf Juergen Kraft, 17, Sam Wagner, 16, sripfoto, 12–13, Standret, cover, Tanya Zima, 19, Viktar Malyshchyts, 15, w.aoki, 4–5, Yuriy Kulik, 6, 8

All internet sites appearing in back matter were available and accurate when this book was sent to press.

Printed and bound in the USA. 4882

Table of Contents

Words in **bold** are in the glossary.

What Are Stars?

Look up at the sky on a clear night. Most of the dots of light you see are **stars**. Stars are huge, glowing balls of bright, hot **gases**. They make their own heat and light.

We usually only see stars at night. They are in the sky during the day too. The sun makes the sky too bright for us to see them.

5

What Are Constellations?

Ursa Major constellation

Groups of stars appear to form patterns. These are called **constellations**. They can look like objects, animals, or people. There are 88 official constellations.

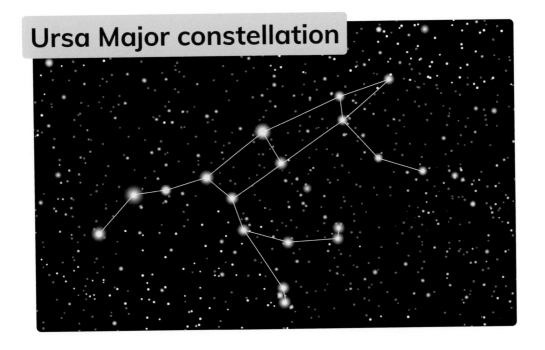

Ursa Major constellation

Some stars in the same constellation might be close together. But most are very far away from each other.

Do Stars Move?

Orion constellation

Find a constellation in the sky. Look again a few hours later. Those stars will be in a different part of the sky. The stars aren't moving. We are!

Earth spins. That makes it seem like stars are moving across the sky. Earth moves around the sun too. That makes constellations move throughout the year.

Do We See Different Stars from Different Parts of Earth?

Yes! There is an imaginary line around Earth. That is the **equator**. It divides our **planet** into two **hemispheres**.

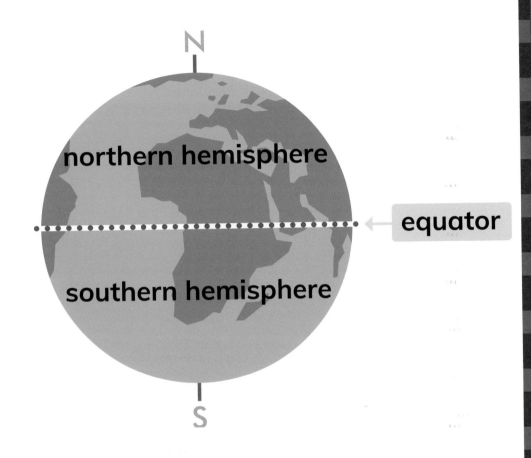

northern hemisphere

equator

southern hemisphere

N

S

What we see in the sky depends on how far north or south of the equator we are. People in different hemispheres see some different stars and constellations.

Why Do Some Stars Look Brighter?

Not all stars are the same! Some are much farther away from Earth than others. Some are even much larger than the sun.

Stars are also different **temperatures**. Some are very hot. That makes them shine brighter. A star much farther away might look brighter. That is because it is likely hotter than a star that is closer to us.

What Are Planets?

Planets are large, round objects that move around the sun. They might look like stars, but they are actually much smaller.

Planets do not give off their own light. They shine because the sun's light **reflects** off them. They look bright because they are much closer to Earth than stars are.

Venus

Jupiter

Do Planets Move?

Watch the same part of the sky at the same time every night. Stars seem to be in the same place. But planets seem to move from night to night.

Jupiter

Planets **revolve** around the sun. Earth also spins. These movements make planets appear in different parts of the sky.

Which Planets Can We See from Earth?

Our **solar system** is made up of the sun and everything that moves around it. That includes Earth and seven other planets.

From Earth, we can see Mercury, Venus, Mars, Jupiter, and Saturn. The other planets are Uranus and Neptune. They are too far from Earth to see without a **telescope**.

Star Light, Star Bright

We need darkness to see the stars in the sky. Try this activity to understand why.

What You Need

- gym (or another large room)

- 2 flashlights

- 2 other people to help

What You Do

1. Stand in one corner of the room with all the lights on. Have one person stand close to you. The other person should stand in the farthest corner.

2. Ask both people to turn on their flashlights and point them toward you. They shouldn't shine in your eyes, just in your direction.

3. Study the flashlights. Do they look bright or dim? Does one light look brighter?

4. Now try turning off all the lights in the room. Repeat steps 2 and 3. Which light looks brighter now?

Just like with the stars, the lights are easier to see in the dark. (With all the lights on, it might be hard to tell if the flashlights are on at all!) But even the same amount of light will look much brighter if it's closer to you.

Glossary

constellation (kahn-stuh-LAY-shuhn)—a group of stars that forms a shape

equator (i-KWAY-tuhr)—an imaginary line around the middle of Earth

gas (GASS)—a substance with no fixed shape that expands to fill any space that holds it

hemisphere (HEM-uhss-fihr)—one half of Earth; the equator divides Earth into northern and southern hemispheres

planet (PLAN-it)—a large object that moves around a star; Earth is a planet

reflect (ri-FLEKT)—to return light from an object

revolve (ri-VOLV)—to turn or to circle around another object

solar system (SOH-lur SISS-tuhm)—the sun and the objects that move around it

star (STAHR)—a large ball of burning gases in space

telescope (TEL-uh-skohp)—a tool people use to look at objects in space; telescopes make objects in space look closer than they really are

temperature (TEM-pur-uh-chur)—how hot or cold something is

Read More

Leed, Percy. *Stars: A First Look*. Minneapolis: Lerner Publications, 2023.

McDonald, Jill. *Exploring the Solar System*. New York: Doubleday Books for Young Readers, 2022.

Nargi, Lela. *Mysteries of the Constellations*. North Mankato, MN: Capstone Press, 2021.

Internet Sites

American Museum of Natural History: A Kid's Guide to Stargazing
amnh.org/explore/ology/astronomy/a-kids-guide-to-stargazing

DK Find Out!: Constellations
dkfindout.com/us/space/constellations

NASA Science: Space Place
spaceplace.nasa.gov/search/stars

Index

About the Author

Thomas K. Adamson has written lots of nonfiction books for kids. Sports, math, science, cool vehicles—a little of everything! When not writing, he likes to hike, watch movies, eat pizza, and of course, read. Tom lives in South Dakota with his wife, two sons, and a Morkie named Moe.